BEHIND THE BRAND
SONY

Sound-from-Picture Reality

BY JOY LAO-SE

BELLWETHER MEDIA • MINNEAPOLIS, MN

Blastoff! Discovery launches a new mission: reading to learn. Filled with facts and features, each book offers you an exciting new world to explore!

This is not an official Sony book. It is not approved by or connected with Sony.

This edition first published in 2025 by Bellwether Media, Inc.

No part of this publication may be reproduced in whole or in part without written permission of the publisher.
For information regarding permission, write to Bellwether Media, Inc., Attention: Permissions Department,
6012 Blue Circle Drive, Minnetonka, MN 55343.

Library of Congress Cataloging-in-Publication Data

Names: Lao-se, Joy, author.
Title: Sony / by Joy Lao-se.
Description: Minneapolis, MN : Bellwether Media, Inc., [2025] | Series: Blastoff! Discovery : Behind the brand | Includes bibliographical references and index. | Audience: Ages 7-12 | Audience: Grades 4-6 | Summary: "Engaging images accompany information about Sony. The combination of high-interest subject matter and narrative text is intended for students in grades 3 through 8"–Provided by publisher.
Identifiers: LCCN 2024046816 (print) | LCCN 2024046817 (ebook) | ISBN 9798893042597 (library binding) | ISBN 9798893044119 (paperback) | ISBN 9798893043563 (ebook)
Subjects: LCSH: Son Kabushiki Kaisha–Juvenile literature. | Electronic industries–Japan–History–Juvenile literature.
Classification: LCC HD9696.A3 J36339 2025 (print) | LCC HD9696.A3 (ebook) | DDC 338.4/76213810952–dc23/eng/20241004
LC record available at https://lccn.loc.gov/2024046816
LC ebook record available at https://lccn.loc.gov/2024046817

Text copyright © 2025 by Bellwether Media, Inc. BLASTOFF! DISCOVERY and associated logos are trademarks and/or registered trademarks of Bellwether Media, Inc.

Editor: Betsy Rathburn   Series Designer: Andrea Schneider   Book Designer: Josh Brink

Printed in the United States of America, North Mankato, MN.

TABLE OF CONTENTS

EVENING ENTERTAINMENT!	4
SONY SETS OUT	6
GAMES AND MORE	18
HELPING OTHERS	26
FUN AND GAMES	28
GLOSSARY	30
TO LEARN MORE	31
INDEX	32

EVENING ENTERTAINMENT!

A boy searches for the perfect movie to watch with his family. He considers *The Karate Kid* and *Hotel Transylvania*. Eventually, he decides on his favorite Sony superhero movie. The family watches *Spider-Man: No Way Home* on their Sony television. The story is exciting, and the television's **resolution** is clear.

Later, the boy fires up his PlayStation 5. There are many fun games to play, including *Marvel's Spider-Man: Miles Morales* and *Astro's Playroom*. He decides to create new worlds on *Dreams*. His whole day was filled with fun Sony products!

SONY SETS OUT

SONY HEADQUARTERS
TOKYO, JAPAN

SONY HEADQUARTERS
NEW YORK CITY

Sony is a company known for its electronics. It makes many different devices such as televisions and cell phones. It is also known for its line of PlayStation **consoles**. The company's main **headquarters** is in Tokyo, Japan. Sony also has a headquarters in New York City.

Sony has several different **divisions**. Sony Pictures Entertainment makes movies. Its Spider-Man series draws big crowds. Sony Interactive Entertainment makes video games. Series such as Spider-Man and Gran Turismo have been successful. Sony offers plenty of exciting electronics and entertainment to fans!

SONY HEADQUARTERS

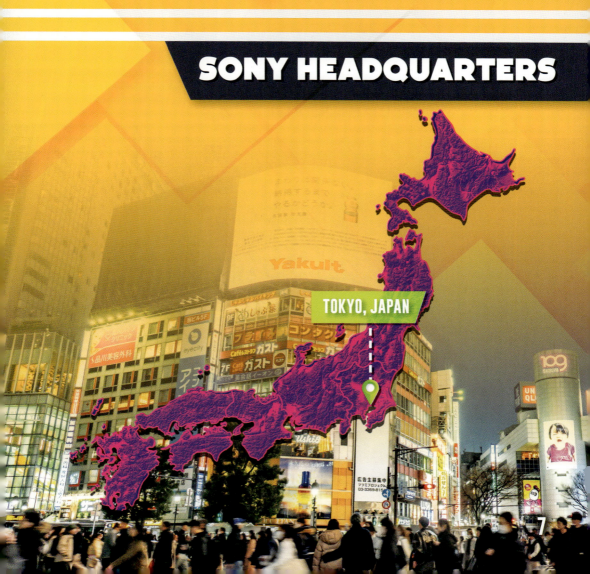

TOKYO, JAPAN

Sony was **founded** on May 7, 1946, in Tokyo, Japan. The company was first called Tokyo Tsushin Kogyo. It was created by two scientists, Masaru Ibuka and Akio Morita. At the time, Japan was rebuilding after World War II. The company mainly repaired radios that had been damaged during the war.

TOKYO AFTER WORLD WAR II

RICE COOKER

The company also wanted to make its own products. Its first product was a simple electric rice cooker. But the results were not consistent. Rice was often cooked poorly. The rice cooker did not sell well.

SONY SOUND

The company name became Sony in 1958. This name is based on the English word *sonny* and the Latin word *sonus*. *Sonus* means "sound."

G-TYPE TAPE RECORDER

In 1950, Sony released the G-type tape recorder. It was the first tape recorder made in Japan. It was not successful. But it led to an improved product, the H-type tape recorder. The H-type's smaller size made it more popular. Many schools bought it!

Sony's first big success came in 1957. The TR-63 was a small **transistor** radio. It could fit in a pocket. Its success made Sony known around the world! In 1960, the company had become so successful that it opened the Sony Corporation of America. Its headquarters was in New York City.

TR-63

SONY FACTORY IN 1962

11

Sony continued to grow its line of products. In 1960, Sony released the TV8-301. This television's screen was only 8 inches (20 centimeters) across! In 1968, Sony released the Trinitron color television. It was very popular. It even won a major award.

TV8-301

1970S TRINITRON TELEVISION

1976 TRINITRON TELEVISION WITH BETAMAX VCR

BETAMAX VCR

This led Sony to make more television-related electronics. In 1971, Sony released its first color VCR. Four years later, Sony released the Betamax VCR. This product greatly improved VCR technology. But it was expensive. It did not sell well. Cheaper but less advanced VCRs continued to be popular for many years.

In 1979, Sony released a portable tape player called the Sony Walkman. This device let people listen to music on the go. It became popular all over the world. Smaller versions were released in 1981 and 1983.

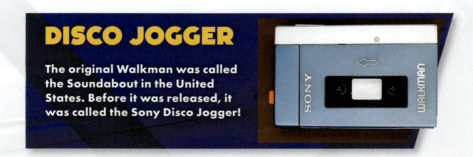

DISCO JOGGER

The original Walkman was called the Soundabout in the United States. Before it was released, it was called the Sony Disco Jogger!

In 1984, Sony introduced the Walkman D-50. It was the first portable CD player. Many more changes came to the Walkman line. Sony even made Walkmans that could play **digital** music. In 2023, the company released new versions with longer battery life and better sound.

WALKMAN DIGITAL MUSIC PLAYERS IN 2012

15

Sound was not the only thing Sony made portable. In 1992, Sony released the Watchman. It was a portable television that fit inside of a pocket. It was discontinued in 2000.

EARLY SONY PRODUCTS

1957	TR-63 TAPE RECORDER
1968	TRINITRON COLOR TELEVISION
1975	BETAMAX VCR
1979	WALKMAN
1985	HANDYCAM

Sony also made products to take photos and record video. In 1981, Sony released the Sony Mavica. This electronic camera stored images on **floppy disks**. It was a type of early digital camera! In 1985, Sony released the Handycam. Its small size made it easy to film videos on the go.

17

GAMES AND MORE

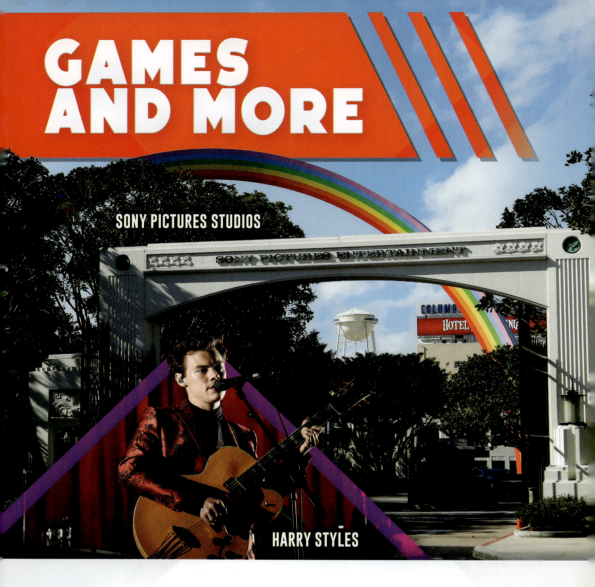

SONY PICTURES STUDIOS

HARRY STYLES

Big changes happened at Sony during the 1980s. In 1982, Norio Ohga became the company's president. He led Sony to buy CBS Records in 1988. Sony gained the **rights** to the music of many famous artists. Some people in the company disagreed with the purchase. They thought Sony should focus on making electronics. Today, Sony continues to release music by popular artists such as Carrie Underwood and Harry Styles.

In 1989, Norio led Sony to buy a movie **studio** called Columbia Pictures Entertainment. Now it is called Sony Pictures Entertainment. Over the years, Sony has released many popular movies!

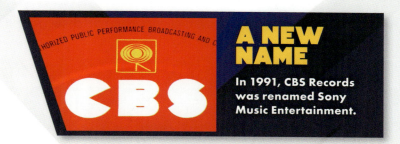

A NEW NAME
In 1991, CBS Records was renamed Sony Music Entertainment.

NORIO OHGA

BORN January 29, 1930, in Numazu, Japan

DIED April 23, 2011

ROLE Former leader of Sony

ACCOMPLISHMENTS Pushed Sony to start creating movies and music

Around this time, video games were gaining popularity. In 1994, Sony released the PlayStation console. Over 102 million sold! The PlayStation launched with several games, including the popular racing game *Ridge Racer*. Later games such as *Gran Turismo* and *Crash Bandicoot* also sold well.

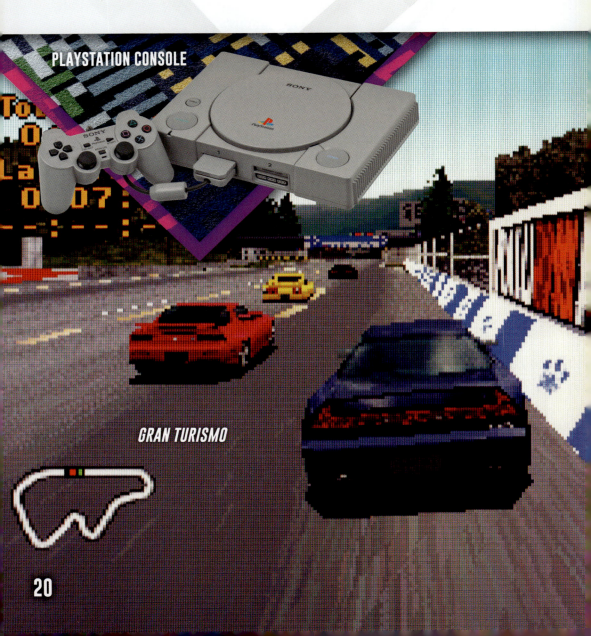

PLAYSTATION CONSOLE

GRAN TURISMO

SONY TIMELINE

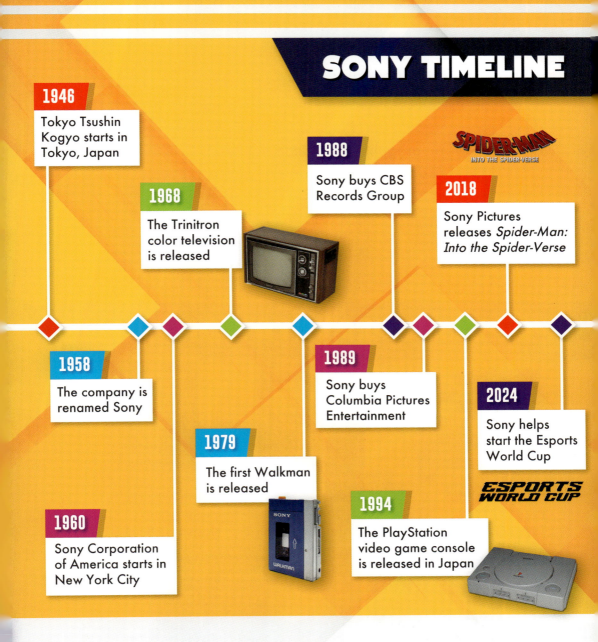

1946 — Tokyo Tsushin Kogyo starts in Tokyo, Japan

1958 — The company is renamed Sony

1960 — Sony Corporation of America starts in New York City

1968 — The Trinitron color television is released

1979 — The first Walkman is released

1988 — Sony buys CBS Records Group

1989 — Sony buys Columbia Pictures Entertainment

1994 — The PlayStation video game console is released in Japan

2018 — Sony Pictures releases *Spider-Man: Into the Spider-Verse*

2024 — Sony helps start the Esports World Cup

In 2000, Sony released the PlayStation 2. It is still the most popular console Sony has ever released. Over 150 million sold! Popular games on this console included *Tony Hawk's Pro Skater 3*, *SSX*, and *Kingdom Hearts*.

21

The PlayStation 3 was released in 2006. More than 87 million sold! Gamers enjoyed new games from the Gran Turismo and Ratchet & Clank series. In 2013, Sony released the PlayStation 4. The 2018 PlayStation 4 game *Marvel's Spider-Man* was popular. It won many awards!

POPULAR PLAYSTATION GAMES

GRAN TURISMO 2
Year: 1999
Console: PlayStation

KINGDOM HEARTS
Year: 2002
Console: PlayStation 2

LITTLEBIGPLANET
Year: 2008
Console: PlayStation 3

MARVEL'S SPIDER-MAN
Year: 2018
Console: PlayStation 4

RATCHET & CLANK: RIFT APART
Year: 2021
Console: PlayStation 5

MARVEL'S SPIDER-MAN: MILES MORALES

In 2020, Sony launched the PlayStation 5. Many fans lined up to buy the console when it was released. Popular games for the console include *Astro Bot* and *Marvel's Spider-Man: Miles Morales*. Fans look forward to new games and consoles from Sony!

HANDHELD!

In 2004, Sony released the PlayStation Portable. This was Sony's first handheld console. Over 80 million sold!

Sony movies have also done well. In 2018, *Spider-Man: Into the Spider-Verse* was released. Many fans liked the movie. It won an **Academy Award** for Best Animated Feature. The **sequel** came out in 2023. *Spider-Man: Across the Spider-Verse* earned over $690 million!

POPULAR SONY MOVIES

	YEAR	BOX OFFICE SALES
CLOUDY WITH A CHANCE OF MEATBALLS	2009	$243,006,136
HOTEL TRANSYLVANIA	2012	$358,375,603
JUMANJI: WELCOME TO THE JUNGLE	2017	$962,544,585
SPIDER-MAN: INTO THE SPIDER-VERSE	2018	$384,298,736
SPIDER-MAN: ACROSS THE SPIDER-VERSE	2023	$690,824,738

JUMANJI: THE NEXT LEVEL

HOTEL TRANSYLVANIA

Other Sony releases have also done well. In 2012, *Hotel Transylvania* was released. Many people love the movie's humor and characters. Several sequels followed. **Live-action** movies are also popular. The Jumanji series has many fans. Movie lovers look forward to the next Sony release!

HELPING OTHERS

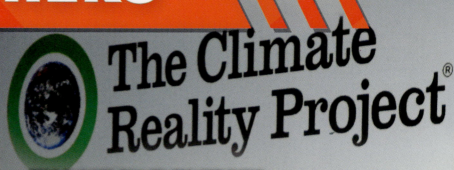

Sony gives back to the community. In 2019, it hosted 11 events about **climate change** with the Climate Reality Project. The events were meant to teach people about climate change and what they can do about it. Sony also started the Sony Global Relief Fund in 2020. It gave $100 million to support people affected by COVID-19.

In 2023, the company gave over $500,000 to help people affected by an **earthquake** in Turkey and Syria. That same year, Sony Music Group gave $500,000 to organizations that help people find food and housing.

GIVING BACK

11 EVENTS
HOSTED WITH THE CLIMATE REALITY PROJECT IN 2019

$100 MILLION
GIVEN TO SUPPORT PEOPLE AFFECTED BY COVID-19

$500,000
GIVEN TO HELP PEOPLE AFFECTED BY AN EARTHQUAKE IN 2023

$500,000
GIVEN TO ORGANIZATIONS THAT HELP PEOPLE FIND FOOD AND HOUSING IN 2023

FUN AND GAMES

Sony fans can attend fun events. Many gather at **conventions** to celebrate favorite games and meet people who created them. Fans often make artwork of favorite characters to sell and share. In 2024, Sony helped start the **Esports** World Cup. Gamers compete in games like *Overwatch* and *Fortnite*. They can win big prizes!

28

Fans of Sony movies can visit movie locations. Sony Pictures does studio tours where people can visit the **sets** of movies like *Spider-Man* and *The Wizard of Oz*! Sony fans have a lot to love about this world-famous **brand**!

ESPORTS WORLD CUP

WHAT IT IS
An esports competition and festival

FIRST HELD
2024

LOCATION
Riyadh, Saudi Arabia

PRIZE POOL
$62.5 million in 2024

GLOSSARY

Academy Award—a yearly award presented for achievement in film; an Academy Award is also called an Oscar.

brand—a category of products all made by the same company

climate change—a human-caused change in Earth's weather due to warming temperatures

consoles—electronic devices mainly used for playing video games

conventions—events where fans of a subject meet

digital—related to electronic or computer technology

divisions—groups within a company

earthquake—an event in which the ground shakes from the movement of Earth's crust

esports—multiplayer video games played in competitions

floppy disks—thin, flexible disks with magnetic coatings that can store information for a computer

founded—started or created

headquarters—a company's main office

live-action—filmed using real actors

resolution—a measurement of the number of pixels that make up a television screen; pixels are the tiny points on a screen.

rights—a legal claim to something

sequel—a movie, game, or other media that continues the story that started in something that came before it

sets—the places where movies or television shows are filmed

studio—a place where movies, video games, or music are made

transistor—related to an electronic device that controls the flow of electricity

TO LEARN MORE

AT THE LIBRARY

Lao-se, Joy. *Microsoft*. Minneapolis, Minn.: Bellwether Media, 2025.

Olson, Elsie. *Electronic Arts*. Minneapolis, Minn.: Bellwether Media, 2025.

Streissguth, Thomas. *Sony: Makers of the PlayStation*. Minneapolis, Minn.: Abdo Publishing, 2024.

ON THE WEB

Factsurfer.com gives you a safe, fun way to find more information.

1. Go to www.factsurfer.com.

2. Enter "Sony" into the search box and click 🔍.

3. Select your book cover to see a list of related content.

INDEX

Betamax VCR, 13
CBS Records, 18, 19
Climate Reality Project, 26
early Sony products, 16
Esports World Cup, 28, 29
fans, 7, 23, 24, 25, 28, 29
giving back, 27
Handycam, 17
Ibuka, Masaru, 8, 9
Morita, Akio, 8, 9
movies, 5, 7, 19, 24, 25, 29
name, 8, 9
New York City, 6, 11
Ohga, Norio, 18, 19
PlayStation, 5, 6, 20, 21, 22, 23
PlayStation Portable, 23
popular PlayStation games, 22
popular Sony movies, 24
radios, 8, 11
sales, 9, 10, 13, 20, 21, 23, 24
Sony Corporation of America, 11
Sony Global Relief Fund, 26
Sony Interactive Entertainment, 7
Sony Mavica, 17
Sony Music Entertainment, 18, 19
Sony Music Group, 27
Sony Pictures Entertainment, 7, 19, 29
tape recorders, 10
televisions, 5, 6, 12, 13, 16
timeline, 21
Tokyo, Japan, 6, 7, 8
video games, 5, 7, 20, 21, 22, 23, 28
Walkman, 14, 15
Watchman, 16, 17
World War II, 8

The images in this book are reproduced through the courtesy of: Miguel Lagoa, front cover (PlayStation 5); Sandor Szmutko, front cover (camera), 19 (camera); Nicola_K_photos, front cover (Walkman); Sorbis, front cover (televisions); Qcon, front cover (phone); victorgeorgiev, front cover (laptop); fnbaihaqi, front cover (PlayStation Vita); aperturesound, front cover (headphones); Sarunyu L, front cover (Miles Morales), p. 31 (Spider-Man); Ink Drop, front cover (PlayStation logo); Poshstocker, p. 2 (Walkman); agencies, p. 3 (PlayStation 5); New Africa, pp. 4-5; Photo 12/ Alamy, p. 5 (*Spider-Man: No Way Home*); Wachiwit, p. 5 (PlayStation 5); Pajor Pawel, p. 6 (Sony headquarters in Tokyo); JHVEPhoto, p. 6 (Sony headquarters in New York City); Byjeng, p. 7 (Tokyo, Japan); Circa Images/ Alamy, p. 8; AP Photo/ Kyodo News/ AP Newsroom, p. 9 (Akio Morita and Masaru Ibuka); Cjchunt/ Wikipedia, p. 9 (rice cooker); monticello, p. 9 (Sony logo); Nippon News/ Alamy, pp. 10, 15 (Walkman D-50), 16 (TR-63); INTERFOTO/ History/ Alamy, p. 11 (TR-63); Mondadori Portfolio/ Getty Images, p. 11 (Sony factory); Aflo Co. Ltd/ Alamy, p. 12 (TV8-301); Science & Society Picture Library/ Getty Images, pp. 12 (Trinitron), 16 (Betamax VCR); Back to the future/ George Arriola/ Wikipedia, p. 13 (Trinitron); AndyHemmerCincinnati/ Wikipedia, p. 13 (Betamax VCR); Trevor Mogg/ Alamy, p. 14 (Walkman display); Chris Willson/ Alamy, p. 14 (1979 Walkman); joho345/ Wikipedia, p. 14 (Disco Jogger); AFP/ Stringer/ Getty Images, p. 15 (digital music players); Bloomberg/ Getty Images, p. 16 (Trinitron); Anna Gerdén/ Wikipedia, p. 16 (Walkman); Holger.Ellgaard/ Wikipedia, p. 16 (Handycamp); Simon/ Flickr, p. 17 (Sony Mavica); Wikipedia, p. 17 (floppy disk); Bettmann/ Getty Images, p. 17 (Watchman); Eric Charbonneau/ Invision/ AP Newsroom, p. 18 (Sony Pictures Studios); Kevin Mazur/ Getty Images, p. 18 (Harry Styles); Ralf Liebhold, p. 19 (CBS logo); Sandor Szmutko, p. 19 (camera); AP Photo/ Richard Drew/ AP Newsroom, p. 19 (Norio Ohga); Evan-Amos/ Wikipedia, p. 20 (PlayStation); ArcadeImages/ Alamy, p. 20 (*Gran Turismo*); Sony/ Wikipedia, p. 21 (Trinitron); Yoshikazu TAKADA f/ Wikipedia, p. 21 (Walkman); Sony Pictures Animation/ Wikipedia, p. 21 (*Spider-Man: Into the Spider-Verse*); Esports World Cup Foundation/ Wikipedia, p. 21 (Esports World Cup logo); Macara/ Wikipedia, p. 21 (PlayStation); Betsy Rathburn, p. 22 (*Gran Turismo 2, Kingdom Hearts*); Cotton_hare/ eBay, p. 22 (*LittleBigPlanet*); Gabe Hilger, pp. 22 (*Marvel's Spider-Man, Ratchet & Clank*), 23 (*Marvel's Spider-Man: Miles Morales*); CFOTO/ Future Publishing/ Getty Images, p. 23 (PlayStation 5 display); AkeForever, p. 23 (PlayStation Portable); TCD/Prod.DB/ Alamy, p. 24 (*Spider-Man: Into the Spider-Verse*); Photo 12, p. 24 (*Hotel Transylvania*); Frank Masi/ Columbia Pictures/ Everett Collection, p. 25 (*Jumanji: The Next Level*); Columbia Pictures/ Everett Collection, p. 25 (*Hotel Transylvania*); AP Photo/Mike Stewart/ AP Newsroom, p. 26 (Climate Reality Project); Matej Kastelic, p. 27 (top left); ElenaR, p. 27 (top right); cn.ycl, p. 27 (bottom left); ungvar, p. 27 (bottom right); Mohammed Saad/ Anadolu/ Getty Images, pp. 28 (Esports World Cup), 29 (Esports World Cup); Vladimka production, p. 28 (*Fortnite*); flowgraph, p. 29 (*Overwatch* character); Birgit Reitz-Hofmann, p. 31 (Walkman); robtek, p. 31 (PlayStation Portable).